THE ART OF

TROMPE L'OEIL
MURALS

THE ART OF
TROMPE L'OEIL
MURALS

Yves Lanthier

NORTH LIGHT BOOKS
CINCINNATI, OHIO
www.artistsnetwork.com

Published by North Light Books, an imprint of F+W Publications, Inc., 4700 E. Galbraith Rd., Cincinnati, Ohio, 45236. (800) 289-0963. First edition.

Other fine North Light Books are available from your local bookstore, art supply store or direct from the publisher.

08 07 06 05 04   5 4 3 2 1

Library of Congress Cataloging-in-Publication Data

Lanthier, Yves
    The art of trompe l'oeil murals / Yves Lanthier.
        p. cm.
    Includes index.
    ISBN 1-58180-552-7 (hc : alk. paper)
    1. Mural painting and decoration --Technique. 2. Decoration and ornament -- Trompe l'oeil. I. Title.

ND2550.L36 2005
                                                        2004050097

Editor: Jennifer Long
Production Coordinator: Kristen Heller
Cover Designer: Leigh Ann Lentz
Interior Designer: Stephanie Strang
Page Designer: Camille DeRhodes
Photographer: Tim Grondin

METRIC CONVERSION CHART

to convert	to	multiply by
Inches	Centimeters	2.54
Centimeters	Inches	0.4
Feet	Centimeters	30.5
Centimeters	Feet	0.03
Yards	Meters	0.9
Meters	Yards	1.1
Sq. Inches	Sq. Centimeters	6.45
Sq. Centimeters	Sq. Inches	0.16
Sq. Feet	Sq. Meters	0.09
Sq. Meters	Sq. Feet	10.8
Sq. Yards	Sq. Meters	0.8
Sq. Meters	Sq. Yards	1.2
Pounds	Kilograms	0.45
Kilograms	Pounds	2.2
Ounces	Grams	28.4
Grams	Ounces	0.04

{ACKNOWLEDGMENTS}

I would like to thank all of my clients—with whom I have become good friends in the process—for allowing me to create my artwork, and for their special relationships with me.

I also want to thank the numerous talented designers that I have worked with who allowed me to create my designs with a free spirit.

Special thanks to yacht designer Robin Rose and her clients, and to designer Laurie Anderson and Art-Glass-Environments, Inc., for the Royal Palm Estate.

I also want to acknowledge photographer Peter Clemmet, who helped me photograph much of my artwork; photographer Shawn McClutcheon for his images of the Wehr Nuts yacht; photographer Tim Grondin; and acquisition editor Maureen Berger. Last but not least, a special thanks to my wife Robin, to my parents, and to my Aunt Carmen for their support.

dedication To all the children.

FOREWORD

WHEN I WAS IN THE FIRST GRADE, my class was asked to draw a person that we liked. Without any thought, I started a portrait of my teacher. (I must admit I had a little crush on her!) To my surprise, almost the entire class was soon surrounding me, admiring my sketch. It was then that I realized I had a gift.

{ I used to stay awake all night exploring the techniques of the old masters } in my wonderful art books, encyclopedias, the Bible—anything I could get my hands on. Sometimes I almost felt as if the masters themselves were there, teaching me and guiding me. (During the day I got caught sleeping through my classes.) At seventeen, totally uninterested in school, I could not see myself growing up to lead a structured life. Feeling my despair, my parents offered me a trip to visit my Aunt Carmen, who was a missionary helping local villagers in the Tamil Nadu region of South India. I stayed there for three months, during which time I did many drawings of temples and old Banyan trees, and completed several oil paintings.

I next traveled to the Himalayas, where I discovered a place called Manaly, or "Valley of God." Here the earth was so rich, the water so pure and the local fruits and vegetables so unbelievable, I felt as if I had never tasted real food before. I stayed there a total of thirteen years. After that I spent three years traveling through Europe; the rich museums and architecture I saw there definitely had an impact on my artwork. In Greece, I sat for hours sketching the ruins and temples, and ended up staying for four months before heading to Amsterdam in 1972. Amsterdam introduced me to the Rembrandt house and Dutch architecture. Munich had exhibitions of van Gogh's earlier works that I had never seen. Later on, Paris and its museums, especially the Louvre and the Salon of the Impressionists, left a great mark on me. The south of France and Italy were also very inspiring.

After spending over fifteen years away from home, I headed back to Canada to see if I could make a living as an artist. At that time, my mother was in the catering business, renting large rooms for weddings and banquets. She was opening a disco downstairs, and this is where I painted my first mural. It was of a woman's face, with her hair running along the entire length of the back walls—a bit visionary and modern, but a mural nonetheless! By then my brother Marc and my sister Lyne both lived in Florida. After living in Asia for so long, I was used to more of a tropical climate than Canada offered, so I bought a car and headed for Florida. I had to make some money, so *{ I started a little painting business. I would wake up around four o'clock in the morning, work on my own painting until eight or nine, and then go to work painting the insides of apartments. Meanwhile, I was looking for a way to start making an income with my art, hoping to place my paintings in some galleries. }*

{One day I answered a newspaper ad calling for painters,} and was hired by a group of French artists working in a Palm Beach mansion. At first I worked on completing areas already started by the other artists, but after a short while I was assigned to create new designs. This really gave me the opportunity to express my creativity. I worked on that project for a year, painting large ceilings and trompe l'oeil doors; handpainting 24k gold leaf details; replicating exotic woods, marble and stone; and designing trompe l'oeil moldings, panels and medallion motifs. It was then time for me to try to succeed by myself. *{I took some photos of the work I had done and started showing them to the design firms in my area.}* It didn't take long before I started picking up work. My first job was a restaurant being opened by a renowned French chef and his partners, and from there numerous jobs followed.

A fortunate encounter led me to my first really big job: at the local library I met an architect who was working for a builder developing several large homes in the Boca Raton area. He suggested I come to the office and show my work. *{They were in need of trompe l'oeil murals in some of the homes they were building. I met with the builder and was hired to paint the model home he had just completed.}*

There was a large rotunda and several other areas that he wanted to be very special, and he was going to showcase them in his advertisements and brochures. This exposure gave me the confidence that I could do or paint anything I wanted to. I was finally able to make a living with my creativity and my art.

CONTENTS

INTRODUCTION

PAGE 10

ROTUNDAS AND DOMES

PAGE 12

CEILINGS AND STAIRCASES

PAGE 32

WALLS AND NICHES

PAGE 46

SOFFITS

PAGE 72

5

DOORS AND DOORWAYS

PAGE 88

6

MURALS ON
CANVAS

PAGE 104

7

TROMPE L'OEIL
PAINTING
TECHNIQUES

PAGE 108

INDEX

PAGE 126

INTRODUCTION

{ *trompe l'oeil* }

FRENCH: *literally, "deceive the eye"*

1: a style of painting in which objects are depicted with photographically realistic detail; also: the use of similar technique in interior decorating.

2: a trompe l'oeil painting or effect.

This book showcases a variety of domes, ceilings, elaborate staircases and murals I custom designed and hand painted for some of the most exquisite estates on the eastern coast of Florida. I hope that browsing through these pages will truly inspire you, whether you're an experienced muralist, or just dream of becoming an artist.

In my large-scale trompe l'oeil painting, I do things differently from other artists, yet I still use the same old methods of large-scale transfer techniques used during the Middle Ages. I can see the same charcoal black dots in closeups of Michelangelo's ceiling details as I use in my own.

I first visualize the general concept in my mind; while painting I compare what I have done to this visualization, and most of the time it turns out just as beautiful as I had projected. Generally, the first idea that comes to mind is most often the best one.

I have travelled throughout the world in my quest for inspiration and knowledge, and you will see some of the results in this book, such as trompe l'oeil statuary and carvings based on what I saw in Italy. Wherever I went I would sketch and paint, and I saw the world like an artist with a blank canvas in front of me. I was ready to create a new style, a new vision, different than ever before.

If you would like to enquire about trompe l'oeil murals, you can contact me at my Web site: http://www.yvesart.com or by phone at (561) 477-5488.

— YVES LANTHIER

STAR ISLAND DOME

This is one of the many preliminary renderings I did for the large dome I painted in an estate on Star Island, Florida. The completed painting is shown on the facing page. Compare this highly detailed rendering of the dome's base and circular window area with the finished painting.

{ROTUNDAS AND DOMES}

In this chapter you will see how trompe l'oeil can be used to emphasize and define such large-scale architectural structures as rotundas and domes. Rather than detailing these areas with plaster or marble, the same effects can be achieved through the use of painted statuary, ironwork, corbels, arches and friezes.

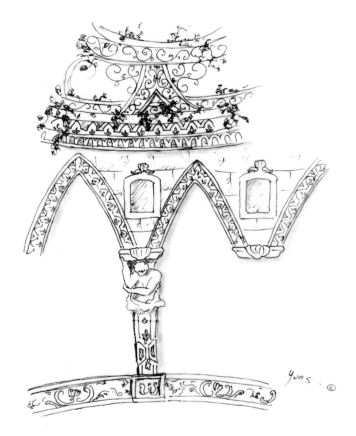

IRONWORK ROTUNDA

When I first started on this project, the house was still under construction, but the potential was obvious. I entered the home through large wooden double doors to find magnificent marble inlay floors throughout. In the foyer there were four stone columns supporting a rotunda. The rotunda had eight openings beneath the windows intended for light fixtures—these had to be planned into my composition. The builder asked me to generate a design for the fixtures and he then had them shaped from resin so I could paint on them. I immediately felt inspired and could visualize the finished painting in my mind. I had a small piece of scrap paper with me so I started shaping some of the forms I had in mind. It was rough but the idea was there and I submitted the drawing shown at left along with my proposal.

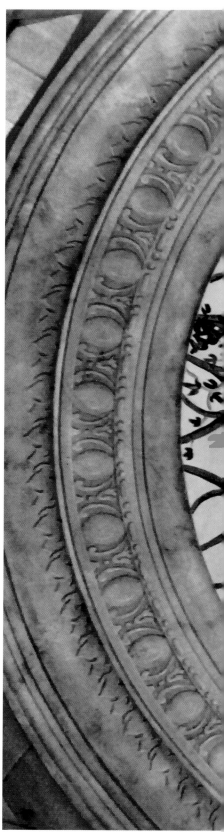

IRONWORK ROTUNDA

{ **before** } Below is a photo of the rotunda as it looked before I started painting.

{ **after** } Part of the challenge of this project was to devise a way to open up the flat ceiling at the apex of the dome. I accomplished this by creating a trompe l'oeil "skylight" with an ironwork design somewhat softened with vines. The first time I went up on the scaffold to sketch in the design, I thought I was in trouble. At close range and with my head at a strange angle, I couldn't make sense of what I was sketching. It was only after laying in the design and coming down onto the floor that I was rewarded with a first glimpse of my artwork in the correct perspective.

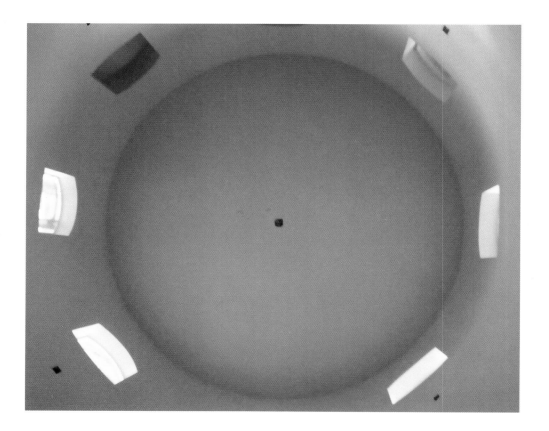

{ detail of statue and border } I took my inspiration for the outside border from a sublime real-life stone carving design, changing the details, shape and colors to make it original. I experimented with washes of gold, red and blue over the faux stone to give it an aged look. Once, while I was working up on the scaffold finishing some details on the border, someone walking by said, "I thought you were putting up wallpaper it looks so perfect." At first I didn't know if that was a compliment or a critique! It took me about a month and a half to paint this dome, from the time I started sketching to completion.

FISHER ISLAND OVAL CEILING

This oval ceiling is part of a large-scale project that encompassed a large coffered ceiling, walls, niches, and corridors. This oval is a focal point when entering the residence, serving as an introduction to what is to come. The patches of sky carry over from the large wall mural, keeping the ornate ceiling from seeming too heavy. The photo on page 19 shows all the interior lights on, and the photo below is with daylight only.

INDIAN CREEK CEILING

A very talented entrepreneur and builder asked me to design this ceiling for his main salon. When I first arrived at his magnificent estate, I could see that it was carefully designed and built with attention to every detail. From the imported marble to the decorative architectural stone details, everything was top of the line. This trompe l'oeil mural covers almost the entire ceiling of the salon, measuring twenty-five feet (seven and one-half meters) square. It took me approximately a month and a half to paint. My inspiration came from a great book on Italian ceilings.

INDIAN CREEK CEILING

Using an antique gold metallic paint for the background of the medallions and for the recessed perimeter helped to add some depth to the ceiling. I created a more domed effect on the flat faux ironwork trellis by adding the same gold highlight at its base and painting the top darker, as if the sunlight were coming from above.

ENTRANCE DOME CEILING

I added the finishing touch to this small entrance dome with a handpainted gold leaf design—detailed with oil paint to create more depth—over a faux background.

STAR ISLAND DOME

This thirty-four foot (10.5 meter) diameter dome took several months to paint. I spent one month at the drawing table just coming up with this design. When I started sketching onto the actual ceiling, I realized this was going to be a real challenge: none of the twelve round windows were placed at the same height or distance from each other. Consequently, every component had to be sketched freehand and stretched in order to carry the pattern around the dome without an obvious variation. I was constantly going up and down the scaffolding to make sure the proportions were correct and nothing appeared crooked from beneath.

STAR ISLAND DOME

Here is how the Star Island dome looked before I began work on it.

{ **sketch** } Above is a sketch of the astral dome in the center of the design.

{ **drawing** } Here is the drawing of the dome base and windows.

MANALAPAN DOME

This thirty-foot (nine meter) diameter dome is located above a circular staircase in the entrance foyer of an estate. When I first saw it, there was a massive copper chandelier at its center, covering a large portion of the dome. When I presented my design (shown below) to the homeowner, I explained to him that I wanted to create something very different and original—an open dome supported by statuary. To emphasize the domed effect, I accentuated the depth perspective of the rosette within the upper architectural dome, making it appear to push even further upward. The owner eventually opted to remove the expensive copper chandelier and install a smaller one to allow a better view of the trompe l'oeil.

STATUARY AND SOFFIT

One sketch served for all the statuary even though at first glance each looks unique. The difference is which arm is raised overhead, right or left, which is achieved just by flopping the sketch.

{ faux marble statuary } This faux marble stonework shown at right is a replica of the actual marble used on the floor underneath this dome. I also incorporated an antique metallic gold accent in certain parts of the background, a technique I developed in previous projects. The lion's head within a circular frame and the floral swags along the soffit are all trompe l'oeil.

{ sketch of lion's head }
The shading along one side helps the lion's head look three-dimensional in the sketch above.

{ CEILINGS AND STAIRCASES }

Trompe l'oeil can be employed to make ceilings that are flat or inset appear to be domed or arched or curved in any way. You'll see several examples of this effect in this chapter, as well as staircase windows where there really are none.

ADMIRAL'S COVE CEILING

The ceiling shown at right is part of a large corridor project I did for a famous Canadian singer. I painted faux stonework on the walls, then, wanting to create a feeling of space in the corridor, I decided to open up the ceiling to a trompe l'oeil sky, complete with iron-work arches and vines. My color rendering of the ironwork concept is shown above.

SPIRAL STAIRCASE

I wanted this staircase, and the ceiling above it, to be simple yet classy. I decided to repeat the arches and stone blocks that I had painted in the home's main rotunda, adding a different stone bracket design. This project presented a few challenges. First, the staircase wall was curved, without a corner, which gave me no clear place to end the stonework. In addition, I didn't have enough space to carry the design over the two smaller top windows. I also had to deal with the fact that the upstairs walls were a different color than the staircase walls, with no demarcation between the two areas. The picture below shows a close-up view of my solution: a simple "crack" in the wall where the stonework ends and the upstairs wall color begins.

SPIRAL STAIRCASE CEILING

Looking straight up at the spiral staircase's ceiling gives the effect that the flat ceiling is domed, but the curved panels and the shading around the bottom edge is what gives that illusion.

ENTRANCE CEILING

Here a simple rectangular shadow and highlight pattern created depth in what would have otherwise been a flat fascia on the beam of this main area ceiling. I added a rosette at each cross intersection for a finishing touch.

ROYAL PALM STAIRCASE

This is one of the most original designs I've come up with. The staircase has a three-sided curved wall with a row of arched windows in the middle; I decided to create trompe l'oeil windows on both sides of the real windows and carry the same painted details around the existing frames of the actual windows. Around the domed ceiling at the top, I simply added faux carved stone details to compliment the artwork beneath.

ROYAL PALM STAIRCASE

The trompe l'oeil architectural details beneath each arched window help fill out this large space very graciously. The "views" out the windows shown on the facing page look upward toward the sky, which is what would be seen by someone standing on the stairs looking out a real window.

ROYAL PALM FLAT CEILING

In this example, I painted a double-tiered flat ceiling to look like a dome opening out to the sky, complete with ironwork and Italian statuary.

TROMPE L'OEIL STATUARY

The perspective of the statuary and architectural elements helps this flat ceiling look domed.

HALLWAY CEILING

I designed this hallway mural to create a more open feel in a tight corridor leading to the master bedroom and bathroom of this home. The ceiling forms a soft arch with a vine-trimmed wood-beamed trellis looking through to the sky. Lighting was strategically placed in back of the trellis so it appears sunlight is shining through from the sky.

On the facing page, you can see the archway entrance into the hallway, with the coved ceiling above it decorated with more vine-trimmed wooden beams.

{WALLS AND NICHES}

Trompe l'oeil painting on flat walls is the most widely known and popular application——it lends itself especially well to scenic vistas where perspective and depth of field are important to the sense of realism. Niches are inset areas of walls where the sides can be brought into play as well.

FISHER ISLAND MURAL

The owners of this home had fallen in love in Italy and wanted a place that reminded them of that precious time. Their entire home is painted with trompe l'oeil to feel like an old Italian castle. This home's front window provided a stunning view of the Atlantic Ocean, so I carried the actual horizon line from the ocean into this painted scene to look like a continuity of the same view. Inspired by the great Italian trompe l'oeil murals, I wanted to create a grand archway with statuary pillars supporting the arches. I chose to create depth by adding a garden leading out toward the ocean. This was one of the most fun projects I've worked on, and the overall accomplishment is one of my favorites. Shown at right is the preliminary sketch for the mural.

FISHER ISLAND MURAL

{ **before** } Shown below is a photo of the room as it looked before I started the mural. Note the cabinet and the large niche along the back wall.

{ **after** } At right, you can see how I visually raised and curved the top of the existing niche to add height and drama to the archway—the opening was originally designed for a dining room buffet. A detail of the statuary is shown on page 50.

{ DETAIL OF }

MURAL STATUARY

This part of the wall mural is to the left of the cabinet and niche shown on page 49. It is entirely trompe l'oeil and even incorporates an electrical outlet and wall switch.

ITALIAN TERRACE WALL MURAL

This hallway mural opens up a fairly narrow corridor. For the composition I worked from an image of a stepped terrace I found in one of my Italian palace books. To change the scene and make it unique, I added the statuary at the end of the garden leading to a cypress allée and the ocean beyond.

CHERUB WITH FLOWER VASE

This panel, one of my first projects as a muralist, adorns a back wall in a French restaurant. I added the colorful flower bouquet to play off the blue, burgundy and gold floral fabric of the decor.

ITALIAN GARDEN FOYER

In this foyer, I painted trompe l'oeil carved stone window niches on either side of the main door. This niche is on the right wall; see page 55 for a close-up view. To tie the niches into the existing architecture, I incorporated the actual stone color and ironwork found in the arched opening nearby.

ITALIAN GARDEN FOYER

The scenes in the two niches are not identical, but the colors I used are, and the horizon lines are the same. I had just returned from Italy when I made my preliminary sketches (see pages 56 and 57), which helped influence the design for these garden scenes. Since these wall murals are seen at very close range, every detail needs to be precise. Being a naturally detailed artist can become challenging when it takes a lot longer than estimated to complete the project. You always have to balance what you want to achieve and how you are going to achieve it.

{ left wall }

{right wall}

ITALIAN GARDEN FOYER

{left wall}

{right wall}

ADMIRAL'S COVE CORRIDOR

I added trompe l'oeil to the walls, doors and ceiling of this corridor, which runs through the center of an estate. Areas that have a lot of different components can be difficult to combine in a smooth, uniform flow. Notice how the door panel design uses the same marble inlay and stone color as the niches on either side. All these little details are what bring uniformity to a design concept.

ADMIRAL'S COVE NICHES

{**boy playing flute**} This is the preliminary
sketch for the niche to the left of the large double doors.

{**girl holding lamb**} This is the sketch
for the niche to the right of the double doors.

CORRIDOR NICHES

{ **boy playing
flute niche** }

This niche is on the left of the
paneled double doors in the
Admiral's Cove corridor (see
photo on page 58). Notice
how the bracket in the upper
corner actually appears to be
protruding from the wall. This
three-dimensional effect is difficult to achieve in a corner.

{girl holding lamb niche}

I always liked the shepherd stories in the Old Testament; I tried to bring some of that essence into these niche statues. This one is to the right of the paneled double doors (see photo on page 58).

61

THE BALCONY SCENE

The corridor wall opposite the niches shown on pages 58-61 is divided by two real half columns. I decided to paint the center portion as an entrance to a balcony leading to a garden, surrounded by faraway mountains. This helps create a depth of field not only for this wall, but also for the entire corridor.

{ **right side panel** } This portion of the corridor wall mural is to the right of the balcony scene shown on the facing page. I added a volute bracket coming down from the top corner to bring curving, harmonic lines to an otherwise boring corner. I also again tied the stone at the bottom to the design under the niches (see pages 60-61).

{ **preliminary sketch** } In this sketch you can see the center portion of the wall mural (shown at right) and the two side portions. The scene under the righthand arch is shown above right.

THE OLD-MAN NICHE

This is another room in the same estate that received trompe l'oeil throughout the walls and ceiling. This wall, located across from a double archway mural, had just enough space for a small niche between two large armoires (see photo on facing page). This niche added just the classical, elegant detail I was looking for. Below, the niche is shown in the larger context of the room.

The "old man" statue was inspired by
an original Versailles garden statue. I
used the same metallic gold throughout the design to create the curved
depth of the niche and highlight the
carved elements.

The cast shadow behind the statue helps "lift" it away from the background and bring it forward in the niche.

BUFFET MURAL

The niche shown on the facing page sits over a built-in buffet in a dining room. I always like to borrow from real-life stone elements in my trompe l'oeil work, and have found the great villas and palaces of Italy to have some of the most exquisite architecture and carved stone details. They were my inspiration for the stone coffered ceiling and column design shown in the mural below.

BUFFET MURAL

{ **before** } Here is what the buffet wall looked like before I started the mural.

{ **after** } The completed mural adds elegance and a feeling of space to the dining room.

{SOFFITS} *As architectural elements, soffits and fascia boards are interesting places to add decorative trompe l'oeil, since they are often quite long and narrow and lend themselves well to friezes that look sculptured, reminiscent of classical Greek temples. Kitchen soffits are the most familiar, but they can also appear in almost any room in the house.*

CLASSICAL KITCHEN

This kitchen soffit was the perfect place for some decorative detailing. The design was inspired by the classical Greek and Roman stone carvings I had always yearned to try my hand at myself one day. Using trompe l'oeil techniques, I was able to create my own carvings with paint instead of a chisel! The preliminary sketch for the figures is shown above.

CLASSICAL KITCHEN SOFFIT

When creating this kitchen soffit design, I had to consider the rounded bottom edge at the front of the soffit. To give the painted panels a more three-dimensional effect, I added a straight edge around the panels with a strong cast shadow underneath. This helped to finish the design, as well as create a transition into the different color at the bottom of the soffit. This was tricky because the curve actually created a shadow of its own that took away from the one I'd painted just above it. I knew my trompe l'oeil was effective when one day I noticed a visiting neighbor raise his hand to touch the soffit to see if it were actually recessed!

DINING ROOM SOFFIT

{ **before** } A few years after I had done some work in this lovely home, the new owner contacted me. He was remodeling certain areas, loved the existing artwork and wanted to do more of the same caliber, maintaining the same style and color palette I'd used in the rest of his home. This dining room soffit was small, but it needed something special to tie it in with all the other beautiful elements in the home. At right is a view of the dining room before I began painting the soffit.

{ **after** } The finished soffit is shown on the facing page. The classical details of the soffit harmonize with the stone columns and marble floors of the home's entrance foyer. →

DINING ROOM SOFFIT

I carried the same stone color and gold metallic paint I had used

elsewhere in the home into the soffit design. I painted the stonework

with a *pochon,* a large stippling brush I had purchased in France.

WHEN PLANNING A PROJECT, I FIRST VISUALIZE THE GENERAL CONCEPT IN MY MIND. IT HELPS

{ *tip* } WHILE PAINTING TO KNOW HOW YOU WISH THE PROJECT TO LOOK WHEN COMPLETED. I FIND THAT THE FIRST IDEA THAT COMES TO MIND IS MOST OFTEN THE BEST ONE. EVEN AFTER SKETCHING FOR HOURS, TRYING DIFFERENT DESIGNS AND

CONCEPTS, I USUALLY COME BACK TO THE FIRST ONE THAT APPEARED IN MY MIND.

DINING ROOM SOFFIT

The arch of the soffit follows the arch of the black cabinetry below, thus emphasizing this interesting detail, and the warm gold background in the trompe l'oeil ties in with the gold on the cabinet doors.

KITCHEN SOFFIT WITH FRUIT GARLAND

Here is another kitchen with a much different feel. To lend weight and importance to the soffit, I painted a stone block design with a decorative border and inset panels of fruit garlands. The simplicity of this design creates an elegant complement to the other aspects of the decor.

FRUIT GARLAND

For this kitchen soffit's center panel, I designed a garland of carved fruit and vegetables, elements that would normally be found in a country kitchen. The garland added life to an otherwise rather plain stone block design.

The colors I used for the lower border design echo the warm tones of the wooden cabinetry and provide a graceful transition between the faux stone block above and the wood below.

TRAILING VINE

Adding a few vines trailing here and there over the soffit helped tremendously in creating a three-dimensional effect. Every little detail counts when you're dealing with a focal point. The holes and cracks in the stone, every molding and edge of the design have to be calculated prior to starting in order to maintain the overall concept balance.

MASTER BEDROOM SOFFIT

There was a very unusual area to be addressed in this master bedroom: a soffit separated the reading area from the rest of the room. Wanting to add a touch of romance, I painted some flowers in the center of the main design. The delicate panel design and rope detail were elegant finishing touches.

MASTER BEDROOM SOFFIT

To soften edges and bring life to the carved stone details of this design, flowers and foliage were used in a swag shape and taken all the way out to the ends, where the leaves on the left side overhang the carving a bit.

{ **side view** } This is the soffit viewed from the entrance to the bedroom. The center panel design is the same as the panels on either side of the flowers on the front of the soffit.

{DOORS AND DOORWAYS} Doors are

wonderful places to paint trompe l'oeil designs, ranging from the simplest of faux paneling to ornate carved pediments. In this chapter you'll see what can be accomplished on doors and arched doorways to create elegant entranceways.

MON PETIT CHOUX

This was one of my first projects, for a high-end French restaurant located in downtown Boca Raton, Florida. I was hired to paint a bread display niche and two panels on the back wall. I created this simple cherub design over the display niche with the letters "MPC" in gold leaf—for *mon petit choux* or "my little darling"—on a blue lapis background for the centerpiece. I remember being so motivated when I started working on this design that I stayed up late into the night sketching the cherubs, got a few hours sleep, then went back on site at 4 a.m. to transfer my design life-size onto the wall without interruption (the restaurant was in a high-profile shopping plaza with a lot of daytime business). The preliminary sketch is shown above. Since this niche was going to display bread, I added some wheat in the right hand of one of the cherubs. The owners liked the design so much, they asked to use it for the menu logo.

GUEST ROOM ENTRANCE

This entrance to a guest bedroom directly faces a spiral staircase I painted with trompe l'oeil stonework and arched windows. Since this door is a major focal point from the stairs, I added a classical design to the doorway to complete the area. This house had so many large areas that could have been painted that I had to concentrate on adding details where they would be most effective and not get lost.

DOORWAY

This was just a little gift for my sister's home where I stayed when I first came to Florida and was begging to paint trompe l'oeil. I wanted to leave her something to remember me by.

Note that the rendering below includes the shadows cast by the architectural elements as if the light were coming from above right. This is important to creating the illusion of depth. Compare this to the finished doorway at left.

I FOUND THAT THE TRICK FOR SUCCESS IS TO ALWAYS BE AHEAD OF THE GAME BY COMING UP WITH NEW, ORIGINAL CONCEPTS AND IDEAS, DIF-FERENT THAN WHAT HAS BEEN DONE BEFORE. I OFTEN

{ *tip* } REFER TO REAL CARVED STONE DETAILS FROM OLD ITALIAN VILLAS OR FRENCH CASTLES TO INCORPORATE IN MY CREATIONS, BRINGING IN DIFFERENT ELEMENTS AND COLORS AND GIV-ING EVEN MORE OF A REALISTIC LOOK.

ARCHED DOORWAY

Separating the entrance and the main ceiling of this large room was an arched area supported by two columns. I thought this would be a perfect place for a beautiful border, accentuating the separation between the two areas.

BATHROOM WALLS

Here you can see how simple decorative borders and faux finishing can transform a space. People generally do not wish to spend a lot of money to decorate their bathroom walls, so a simple yet elegant treatment was important to stay within the allowed budget for this project.

BATHROOM DOORWAYS

This bathroom includes several doors; rather than detailing all of them, I simply added a carved stone detail above these two smaller doors, which are the focal point when entering the bathroom. This artistic touch tied the doors in with the beautiful painted details above the mirror (shown on facing page), while allowing me to leave the other doors plain and simple.

CARVED STONE DESIGN

To create great trompe l'oeil and make it look like a million bucks on a small budget, you have to add very explicit, fine details at focal point areas, decide how much detail you can elaborate on, and where it can be placed most effectively. The photo below shows one of my main focal points—the large painted design above the bathroom mirror.

{ detail of carved stone design } One of the most important hallmarks of good trompe l'oeil painting is shown clearly in this detail: highlights and cast shadows that are consistent with the light source throughout the design.

{**rendering for carved stone design**} Even on a preliminary rendering such as this one, it is important to decide where your light source is, then keep your highlights and shadows consistent. Errors in this regard will be apparent in the finished painting and will reduce the effect of realism and depth of field.

CORRIDOR DOORS

The doors shown on the facing page are found in the Admiral's Cove corridor illustrated on pages 58-63. The door design is a combination of Arabic and classical influences, and uses the same marble inlay and stone color as the niches flanking it. Above the door, the corridor opens up to a trompe l'oeil trellis and the "sky" beyond. On this page is the rendering I made when planning this design.

DINING ROOM DOORWAY

The entrance to this dining room, located at the base of a staircase, was a perfect area to add decorative detail. It is here that visitors get a first glimpse of artwork when coming into the home. I repeated the pattern I had painted around the staircase window on the side of the door frame, then elaborated by adding corbels and different carved details at the top. This changed the plain wall and doorway into a very elegant entrance that makes one wonder what comes next.

{MURALS ON CANVAS}

Painting murals on canvas has several advantages over painting them directly onto walls, ceilings, or other fixed surfaces. First, they're portable—if you (or your clients) move, they can be taken with you. They're also easier to work on; you can complete the mural in the comfort of your own studio. And you don't have to set up scaffolding or work from high ladders. They're a great way to get started in trompe l'oeil mural painting—if you don't like what you've done, just roll up the canvas, put it away and try again.

BOUGAINVILLEA TRELLIS

This 8' x 11' (2.5m x 3.5m) mural on the facing page was painted on canvas which was then glued directly into a wall niche. Living on the east coast of Florida, it was easy for me to imagine this landscape. The angles of the overhead beams of the trellis and the narrowing walkway help give a sense of perspective and depth of field. The preliminary sketch for this mural is shown at right.

NAPOLI MONUMENT

This was an actual white marble monument I saw while traveling through the city of Napoli, Italy. It inspired me to create this mural in oils on canvas. Note how many colors there are in "white" marble. Only the portions of the monument being lit directly by the brightest sunlight are truly white. The rest are pinks, blues, grays and browns.

THE OTHER SIDE

Yacht designer Robin Rose asked me to paint this original oil mural on canvas to go at the end of a corridor in one of the yachts she was working on. The idea was to create an opening at the end of the corridor leading to the four guest staterooms located below deck. This was an ideal location to create a scene that seems to break through the wall—a scene one might encounter on board a yacht as it came into a cove somewhere on the southern coast. The arched rock formation in the foreground provided the uneven opening needed to lengthen and brighten the end of the corridor, while the water gave a feeling of depth.

{TROMPE L'OEIL PAINTING TECHNIQUES}

This chapter will teach you some basic techniques of trompe l'oeil painting through four step-by-step demonstrations of simple decorative elements. Use these elements alone or in combination to add an elegant artistic touch to your home decor, or adapt the techniques to your own designs for a look that's uniquely yours.

ORNAMENTAL PANEL

The first step-by-step demonstration starting on page 110 will show you how to paint the ornamental panels with the gold background below the window sill in the design at right. Demonstration 2 on pages 115-117 shows how to paint the little rosette in the center between the two panels. To see this ornamental panel in context of the full mural, refer to the circular staircase on pages 39-41.

ORNAMENTAL PANEL

In this demonstration, you'll learn how to paint a simple design of scrolls and leaves within a frame. To keep the frame parallel and square, you may want to measure and draw two horizontal lines within which to place the pattern shown below.

step 1

Transfer this pattern onto your basecoated surface with a pencil. Keep in mind that the sketch will show through the entire painting process, so the pencil lines must be light.

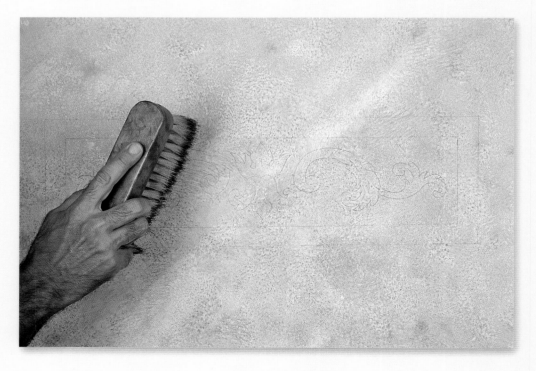

step 2

Wash the background color over your surface. While it's still wet, stipple all over your surface using a large stippling brush. Then "slip-slap" the brush lightly on the stippled paint to soften the finish.

step 3

Flyspeck your surface a bit with a darker color. Load a brush with a little paint and flick the bristles lightly toward the surface. If the flyspecks are too large, you have too much paint in the brush or you are too close.

step 4

With a small round brush, add a little veining with a darker color. This shouldn't be too pronounced (as in marbling), just a subtle bit of veining to mimic the imperfections of natural stone.

step 5

Paint a translucent layer of antique gold over the background of the panel, making sure the stone finish shows through.

{ *tip* } I WORK WITH TRANSLUCENT LAYERS AND WASHES OF PAINT TO ACHIEVE SUBTLETY IN MY MURALS. I USE ACRYLIC PAINTS BECAUSE THEY DRY QUICKLY, BUT MY TECHNIQUE IS CLOSER TO THAT OF OIL PAINTING.

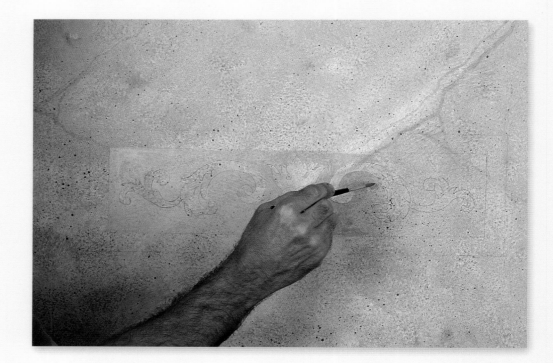

step 6

For the first layer of shading, take a small flat brush and apply a translucent layer of shadow to the outside and underside edges of your design elements. Pick a direction for your light source and keep your shading consistent with that direction.

step 7

Now deepen the shadows a second time. This will create depth in your design, which is one of the most important hallmarks of trompe l'oeil painting.

{ *tip* } IT'S IMPORTANT TO WAIT UNTIL EACH LAYER OF PAINT DRIES. YOU CAN USE A SMALL HAIR DRYER TO SPEED THE DRYING PROCESS. OTHERWISE, YOU WILL PULL OFF THE PAINT FROM THE PREVIOUS LAYER, CREATING A HOLE WHICH IS DIFFICULT TO CORRECT.

step 8

With a small round brush, apply highlights to your details with translucent white. Think about the direction of your light source and keep the highlights consistent to carry the illusion throughout the design.

step 9

In order to make the highlights stand out more three-dimensionally
in areas where there are no shadows, add a small shadow above the
highlights to create contrast.

ROSETTE

Rosettes are one of the most widely used architectural elements in the world. Almost any important building designed in the last few hundred years will have rosettes as part of its ornamentation. Here is a simple one to get you started.

step 1

Trace this pattern and transfer it to your basecoated surface using a pencil. Keep your lines light as they will show through the painting if they're too dark.

step 2

Wash the background color over your surface. While it's still wet, stipple all over your surface with a large stippling brush. Now "slip-slap" the brush lightly over the surface to soften the finish. Flyspeck your surface a bit with a darker color.

step 3

With a small round brush, add a little veining with a darker color. This shouldn't be too pronounced (as in marbling), just a subtle bit of veining to mimic the imperfections of natural stone.

step 4

For the first layer of shading, decide the direction of your light source, then take a small flat brush and apply a translucent layer of shadow to the outside and underside edges of the rosette. Let dry.

step 5
Deepen the shadows a second time. This will create the illusion of depth in your design.

step 6
With a small round brush, apply highlights to the rosette with translucent white. Keep the placement of the highlights consistent with the direction of the light source.

CLASSICAL BORDER

In this demonstration you'll learn how to take one design element and repeat it as often as needed to make one continuous border. This border was used on the kitchen soffit shown on pages 81-84, but here I've added a little color as an accent.

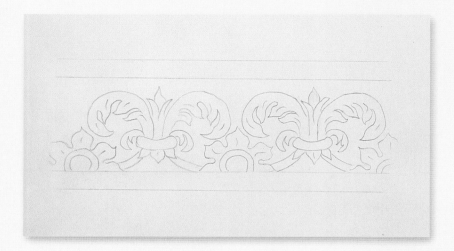

step 1

Trace the pattern at left and transfer it to your basecoated surface using a regular pencil. Keep your pencil lines light—dark lines will show through the paint.

step 2

You can use any faux finish you like as a background for this border. Here I am using a stone finish. A faux marble finish would also work well.

Wash the background color over your surface. While it's still wet, using a large stippling brush, stipple all over your surface. Then "slip-slap" the brush lightly on the stippled paint to soften the finish. Flyspeck your surface a bit with a darker color. Load a brush with a little paint and flick the bristles lightly toward the surface. If the flyspecks are too large, you have too much paint in the brush or you are too close.

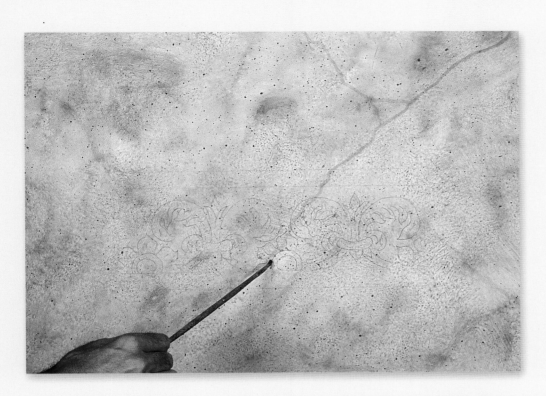

step 3

With a small round brush, add a little veining with a darker color. This shouldn't be too pronounced, just a subtle bit of veining to mimic the imperfections of natural stone.

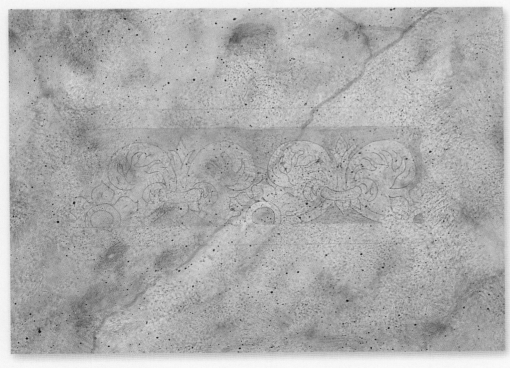

step 4

Apply antique gold acrylic paint to the background of the design.

step 5

Using a small round brush and a color wash of blue, accent part of the design. Accent the other parts with a color wash of red.

step 6

Load a small flat brush with a thinned dark color and place shadows on the border. Decide from which direction your light source is coming, and place the shadows accordingly. Let dry.

step 7

Go over the shadows again to darken them. Re-apply the darker color with a finer brush to make the shadows more exact.

step 8

With a small round brush, apply highlights with translucent white. Keep the placement of the highlights consistent with the direction of the light source.

ORNAMENTAL SHELL

An ornamental shell is a very usable design, especially centered over areas like doors and niches. The shell itself gives height, while the scrolls and leaves to the sides give as much width as you need.

step 1

Trace the pattern at left and transfer it to your basecoated surface using light pencil lines.

step 2

Wash the background color over your surface. While it's still wet, using a large stippling brush, stipple all over your surface. Then "slip-slap" the brush lightly on the stippled paint to soften the finish. Fly-speck your surface a bit with a darker color. Load a brush with a little paint and flick the bristles lightly toward the surface. With a small round brush, add a little veining with a darker color.

step 3

With a watery wash of the shadow color loaded onto a medium flat brush, fill in the shadow details of the scalloped shell shape. Before painting in the shadows, decide from which direction your light source is coming, and keep the shadows consistent.

step 4

Deepen the design elements of the shell once again with a medium flat brush and a dark wash.

step 5

With a smaller round brush, darken the details in the shell more precisely. Notice that the light source is to the right. It's important in trompe l'oeil to keep the light source consistent to create the illusion of depth.

step 6

Highlight the shell with translucent white on a small round brush. Again, think of where your light source is and keep the highlights consistent.

step 7

Finish by deepening any areas where the shadows need further defining to help "lift" the shell design away from the background.

ONE OF THE MOST TIME-CONSUMING BUT IMPORTANT ASPECTS OF PAINTING MURALS IS MIXING YOUR COLORS. WHEN I AM ON A JOB SITE, I USUALLY MIX MORE COLOR THAN I THINK I AM GOING TO NEED. YOU NEVER KNOW

{ *tip* } WHEN A CLIENT IS GOING TO REQUEST THAT YOU ADD ELEMENTS TO YOUR DESIGN. THIS WAY, YOU WON'T NEED TO SPEND TIME MIXING THE COLORS AGAIN.

THAT BEING SAID, I ALSO KEEP A RECORD OF THE PROPORTIONS OF COLORS I USE TO CREATE EACH MIX IN CASE I DO NEED TO MAKE MORE AT A LATER DATE.

INDEX

{ a }

Accenting, 120
Admiral's Cove ceiling, 32-33
Admiral's Cove corridor, 58-63
Arched ceiling, 44
Arched doorway, 94

{ b }

Background color, 110, 115, 122
Balcony scene, 62-63
   See also Garden scenes, Terrace scene
Bathroom doorways, 96-99
Bathroom walls, 95
Border
   classical, 118-121
   and statue, 17
Bougainvillea trellis, 104-105
Boy playing flute, 59-60
Buffet mural, 68-71

{ c }

Canvas, murals on, 104-107
Ceiling
   entrance, creating depth, 37
   entrance dome, 23
   flat, giving dome illusion, 42-43
   hallway, 44
   oval, 18-19
   salon, 20-22
   with sky, ironwork, and vines, 32-33
   spiral staircase, 36
   See also Dome
Chandelier, 28-29

Cherubs, 88-89
   with flower vase, 52
Classical kitchen soffit, 72-75
Colors
   demarcation between areas, 34
   mixing, 125
Corbel statues, 16-17
Corridor
   Admiral's Cove, 58-63
   doors, 100-101
Cove scene, 107
Curved surfaces
   soffit, 76-80
   soffit edge, 74
   staircase walls, 34-35, 38-41

{ d }

Design
   bringing uniformity to, 58
   carved stone, 96-99
   finding new concepts and ideas, 93
   perspective and, 14
Design challenges
   creating demarcation between colors, 34
   curved-edge soffit, 74
   irregularly placed windows, 24
Details, 97
Dining room
   doorway, 102-103
   soffit, 76-80
Dome
   creating illusion of, 36, 42-43
   entrance, 23

   open, with statuary, 28-31
   and rotunda, 12-17
   with windows, 24-27
Doors, corridor, 100-101
Doorways, 88
   arched, 94
   bathroom, 96-99
   creating depth, 92-93
   dining room, 102-103
   guest room, 90-91
Drying, 113

{ e }

Entrance ceiling
   creating depth, 37
   dome, 23

{ f }

Faux finish, background, 118
Faux marble statuary, 30
Fisher Island mural, 46-50
Fisher Island oval ceiling, 18-19
Flowers and foliage, 85-86
Flower vase, 52, 90-91
Flyspecking, 111, 115, 118, 122
Foyer, Italian garden, 53-57
Fruit garland, 81-84

{ g }

Garden scenes, 46-47, 49, 53-57, 104-105
Girl holding lamb, 59, 61
Guest room entrance, 90-91

{ h - i }

Hallway

    ceiling, 44

    Italian terrace mural, 51

    See also Corridor

Highlights, 98-99, 113, 117, 121, 124

Indian Creek ceiling, 20-22

Ironwork rotunda, 12-15

Italian garden foyer, 53-57

Italian themes, 46

{ k - l }

Kitchen soffits

    classical, 72-75

    with fruit garland, 81-84

Light source. *See* Highlights, applying; Shading

Lion's head, 30

{ m }

Manalapan dome, 28-31

Marble, colors in, 106

Master bedroom soffit, 85-87

Mural(s)

    buffet, 68-71

    on canvas, 104-107

    Fisher Island, 46-50

    Italian terrace wall, 51

{ n }

Napoli monument, 106

Niche(s)

    adding height and drama to, 48-49

    Admiral's Cove, 59-61

bread display, 88-89

built-in buffet, 68-71

carved stone window, 53-57

"old man" statue, 64-67

{ o - p }

Ornamental panels, 108-114

Ornamental shell, 122-125

Oval ceiling, 18-19

Paint, translucent layers and washes, 112

Painting techniques, 108-109

Panel, cherub with flower vase, 52

Pattern, transferring, 110, 115, 118, 122

Pochon, 78

{ r }

Rosette, 115-117

Rotunda, ironwork, 12-15

Royal Palm flat ceiling, 42-43

Royal Palm staircase, 38-41

{ s }

Shading, 112-113, 116-117, 120-121, 123-125

Shadows

    cast, 98-99

    creating depth with, 92-93

Shell, ornamental, 122-125

Soffit(s), 72

    dining room, 76-80

    master bedroom, 85-87

    statuary and, 30

Soffit, kitchen

    classical, 72-75

with fruit and garland, 81-84

Spiral staircase, 34-35

Staircase

    Royal Palm, 38-41

    spiral, 34-35

Star Island dome, 24-27

Statuary

    corbel, 16-17

    creating domed illusion with, 43

    faux marble, 30

    mural, 50

    Napoli monument, 106

    niche, 64-67

Stippling, 110, 115, 118, 122

Stone elements, borrowing, 68

{ t }

Terrace scene, 51

Trompe l'oeil

    defined, 11

    painting techniques, 108-109

{ v - w }

Veining, 111, 116, 119, 122

Vine

    with sky and ironwork, 32-33, 44

    trailing, 84

Volute bracket, 62

Walls

    bathroom, 95

    curved, 34-35, 38-41

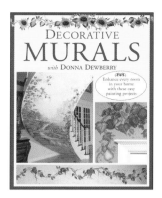

THE BEST IN HOME DECORATING INSTRUCTION AND INSPIRATION IS FROM NORTH LIGHT BOOKS!

Decorative Murals with Donna Dewberry

Step by step, acclaimed decorative artist Donna Dewberry shares some of her favorite tricks and techniques for creating trompe l'oeil murals, floral designs, faux finishes, popular theme designs and more. Donna's clear and encouraging instruction is filled with expert tips for doing each job a little faster and easier, along with answers to common questions about surface preparation, tools and paints! The hardest part will be deciding which gorgeous effect you want to paint first.

ISBN 0-89134-988-X, paperback, 144 pages, #31459-K

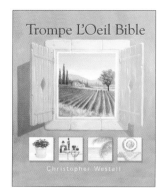

Trompe L'Oeil Bible

Discover a unique collection of original and inspirational trompe l'oeil motifs ideal for any home. You'll find everything you need to capture the perfect scene, from country pitcher on a shelf or climbing wisteria to curtains surrounding a window or a Greek landscape glimpsed through a marble arch. Designs include country views with a Provence landscape, classical views with Greek landscape, water's edge view featuring a sea-inspired landscape and more!

ISBN 0-7153-1479-3, paperback, 128 pages, #41568-K

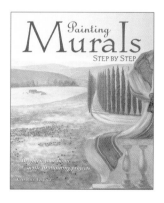

Painting Murals Step-by-Step

Charles Grund takes the fear out of painting large, beautiful murals that fool the eye and stir the soul. Full color, step-by-step instructions provide you with the confidence and control you need to design and painting amazing wall murals. You'll find eleven projects with a variety of themes suitable for almost any room.

ISBN 1-58180-141-6, paperback, 144 pages, #31890-K

Trompe L'Oeil Murals Using Stencils

Learn how to create stunning illusions on walls, floors, and ceilings. Here's all the instruction you need to use inexpensive, laser-cut plastic stencils with skill and confidence. Author Melanie Royals shows you how to combine stencils, shields, and tape with simple paint techniques, buy the proper equipment, prepare surfaces, manipulate stencils, and apply paint. The final section provides more advanced instruction for large-scale projects.

ISBN 1-58180-028-2, paperback, 128 pages, #31668-K

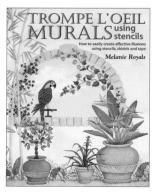

These books and other fine North Light titles are available from your local art & craft retailer, bookstore, online supplier or by calling 1-800-448-0915.